14th International Joint Conference on Natural Language Processing and the 4th Conference of the Asia-Pacific Chapter of the Association for Computational Linguistics (IJCNLP-AACL 2025)

Tutorial Abstracts

Mumbai, India
20-24 December 2025

ISBN: 979-8-3313-3248-8

Printed from e-media with permission by:

Curran Associates, Inc.
57 Morehouse Lane
Red Hook, NY 12571

Some format issues inherent in the e-media version may also appear in this print version.

Association for Computational Linguistics
209 N. Eighth Street
Stroudsburg, Pennsylvania 18360

Phone: 1-570-476-8006
Fax: 1-570-476-0860

acl@aclweb.org

Additional copies of this publication are available from:

Curran Associates, Inc.
57 Morehouse Lane
Red Hook, NY 12571 USA
Phone: 845-758-0400
Fax: 845-758-2633
Email: curran@proceedings.com
Web: www.proceedings.com

IJCNLP-AACL 2025

The 14th International Joint Conference on Natural Language Processing and the 4th Conference of the Asia-Pacific Chapter of the Association for Computational Linguistics

Proceedings of the Conference (Tutorial Abstracts)

December 20-24, 2025

Message from the Tutorial Chairs

Welcome to the tutorial session of IJCNLP-AACL 2025!
This year's tutorials provide focused introductions to a range of developing and established topics in natural language processing and computational linguistics. They are intended to support both newcomers and experienced researchers by offering clear overviews, methodological insights, and perspectives on current directions in the field.
We received 13 tutorial proposals, which were evaluated based on originality and potential impact, anticipated participant interest, the expertise of the instructors, and contributions to the diversity of the conference. Following review and discussion, we selected 6 proposals for inclusion in the program.
We thank all proposers for their submissions, as well as the members of the organizing committee, volunteers and Underline staff for making this tutorial session possible.
We hope the tutorials contribute meaningfully to your experience at IJCNLP-AACL 2025.

IJCNLP-AACL 2025 Tutorial Chairs
Benjamin Heinzerling and Lun-Wei Ku

Table of Contents

Source Attribution for Large Language Models

Vipula Rawte[2], Koustava Goswami[1], Puneet Mathur[1], Nedim Lipka[1]

[1]Adobe Research [2]Adobe Inc.
vrawte@adobe.com

Abstract

As Large Language Models (LLMs) become more widely used for tasks like document summarization, question answering, and information extraction, improving their trustworthiness and interpretability has become increasingly important. One key strategy for achieving this is **attribution**, a process that tracks the sources of the generated responses. This tutorial will explore various attribution techniques, including model-driven attribution, post-retrieval answering, and post-generation attribution. We will also discuss the challenges involved in implementing these approaches, and also look at the advanced topics such as model-based attribution for complex cases, table attribution, multimodal attribution, and multilingual attribution.

1 Introduction

In the context of LLMs, attribution refers to the process of identifying and linking the information generated by the model to its original sources. This involves tracing the content produced by the LLM back to the specific documents, datasets, or other reference materials that informed the response. The goal of attribution is to provide transparency, verify the accuracy of the information, and give credit to the original authors or sources. This is particularly important for ensuring the trustworthiness and accountability of the outputs from generative AI systems.

Attribution methods are pivotal in enhancing the trustworthiness and interpretability of LLMs. They substantiate the model's claims with evidence in the form of references or citations, promoting accuracy and reducing misinformation risk. This ensures each statement produced by the model is backed by appropriate references, establishing a framework for evaluating the completeness and relevance of supporting evidence.

Research in attribution methods for LLMs includes techniques for citation generation, claim verification, and hallucination detection. These techniques aim to improve the quality and trustworthiness of the content generated by LLMs. However, implementing attribution methods in LLMs presents challenges. These include the need for robust validation measures, addressing sources used in reasoning but not present in the final output text, dealing with structured sources or sources in other modalities such as tables or figures and images, and dealing with multi- or cross-lingual sources. Overcoming these challenges is crucial for the successful application of attribution methods in LLMs.

As reliance on AI and machine learning models continues to grow, the need for accountability, transparency, and trustworthiness becomes increasingly important. Attribution methods provide a means to achieve these objectives, making them an essential area of study and application in our community and beyond. This tutorial provides an introduction to the problem space and existing work. We'll dive into areas such as model-based attribution for challenging cases, table attribution, multimodal attribution, and multilingual attribution.

2 Outline

1. Background and existing work (see Section 4) (40 mins)
2. Model-based approaches for post-generation attribution (see Section 5) (40 mins)
3. Tabular attribution (see Section 6) (40 mins)
4. Multimodal attribution (see Section 7) (40 mins)
5. Multilingual attribution (see Section 8) (25 mins)
6. Attribution and factuality (see Section 9) (25 mins)

Proceedings of the 14th International Joint Conference on Natural Language Processing and the 4th Conference of the Asia-Pacific Chapter of the Association for Computational Linguistics: Tutorial Abstract, pages 1–5
December 20-24, 2025

3 Target Audience

This tutorial is designed for AI practitioners and researchers who are interested in understanding the landscape of current attribution approaches and designing solutions for generative AI for knowledge workers. The tutorial aims to inspire new research and benchmark creation through the discussion of several open challenges.

To get the most out of this tutorial, attendees should have:

- Basic knowledge about LLMs: Understanding the fundamental concepts of LLMs will help attendees grasp the attribution approaches discussed in the tutorial.
- Familiarity with Information Retrieval: Knowledge of information retrieval techniques will be beneficial as these methods are often used in conjunction with LLMs.

Approximate count: 30-50. Additionally, the tutorial is designed to accommodate a wide range of participants, from those new to the field to experienced practitioners and researchers. The tutorial's content will be beneficial to all attendees, regardless of their level of expertise.

4 Background and existing work

Attribution methods for LLMs in the field of NLP can be categorized based on their approach: (i) direct model-driven attribution, (ii) post-retrieval answering, and (iii) post-generation attribution (Li et al., 2023). We will provide examples for each approach and discuss their nuances, potential, and challenges.

5 Model-based approaches for post-generation attribution

Current post-attribution technologies are challenged by "hard cases" where the generated responses infer new information not explicitly present in the provided content, such as generated opinions, calculation results, logical deductions, comparisons, etc. In response to this challenge, we will explore the "implicit" reasoning within an LLM, investigating attentions and activation patterns to gain insights into how the model processes and generates information. We will also examine the intersection between source attribution and a phenomenon known as "hallucination" in LLMs.

6 Tabular attribution

Tables are widely used for handling complex semi-structured data in various domains, including healthcare, finance, and education. Application of LLMs to tabular data presents unique challenges: hierarchical header structures, varying formats (e.g., JSON, HTML, CSV, Markdown), lack of straightforward serialization techniques, noisy content, and ambiguity in raw data (e.g., abbreviations, domain-specific terms) (Sui et al., 2023). Due to the high specificity of table data, attributing table structures at the row/column level in generated answers remains under-explored. Prior methods for post-hoc answer attribution use embedding-based retrievers or LLM prompting that are limited to attributing entire tables rather than fine-grained structures (Huo et al., 2023).

We will introduce a novel task, `Fast-Tab: Fine-grained Attribution over Structured Tables` which involves identifying table rows and columns that directly support claims in a generated answer to a user's question. Next, we will discuss existing baseline methods for this new task. Finally, we will expand on our novel agentic framework – `MATSA: Multi-Agent Table Structure Attribution`, that provides inline citations for generated answers based on table structures by coordinating multiple LLM agents.

7 Multimodal attribution

When we talk about long documents, often the documents consist of figures, charts, and images along with long text paragraphs. In many cases, the answers to the asked questions might have a contextual link to localized parts of the images along with a connection to the textual passages. In ideal cases, a multimodal attribution system should be able to cite the sentences back to both images and texts. While textual attribution systems in post-hoc settings are improved with the introduction of high-quality embedding and language models, multimodal attribution is still pretty much new and unexplored. Discussing images is not very straightforward; the images can have noisy content, overlapping contents which make it hard to read, and noisy textual contents in the images. Moreover in the case of charts, depending on the types, the textual contents might be overlapping making it hard to be localized. Prior methodology in text-image space has explored the Referring Expression Segmentation task but does not deal with long textual contexts to be attributed along with the localized image parts. Thus, we will be introducing a new task called multimodal attribution which supports long documents having charts, info-graphics, and natural images.

With the recent advancements in multimodal models, we will explore the potential of leveraging these capabilities to simultaneously attribute generated text to multiple input modalities.

8 Multilingual attribution

We will discuss the challenges faced when dealing with multiple languages, especially those that are under-resourced in terms of data and model training. We will also discuss the complexities that arise in a cross-lingual setup where the languages of the source document, query, and answer are different.

9 Attribution and factuality

Attribution can help mitigate hallucinations in LLMs. Ensuring that responses include citations to reliable sources can help verify the information. By referencing specific articles, studies, or databases, the model's outputs can be cross-checked for accuracy.

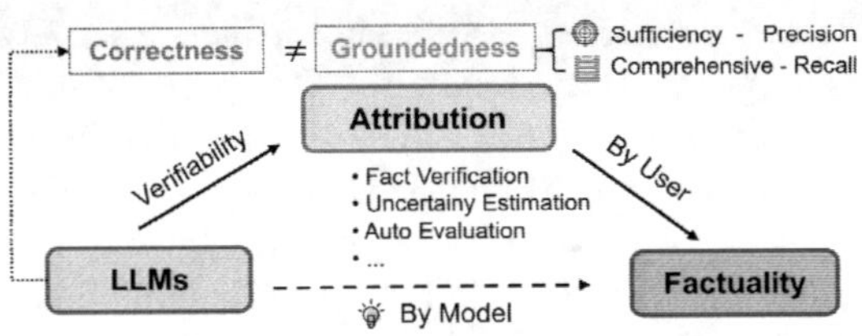

Figure 1: Using attribution for fact-checking (Li et al., 2023).

In the above Fig. 1, using attribution can help developers, and users see the potential sources of an answer and assess its factuality and reliability, enabling them to form their own judgments. Attribution provides a practical approach to reducing hallucinations, as it circumvents the challenge of directly verifying the "truthfulness" of statements, which is often difficult except for the simplest queries.

10 Diversity Considerations

The topic of this tutorial is highly relevant to producing verifiable and trustworthy generative outputs that assist knowledge workers and consumers in navigating information. By focusing on attribution approaches, we aim to contribute to responsible and grounded AI solutions.

While the topic is not specifically targeted at a particular underrepresented group, it is universally applicable to all potential participants. However, we will encourage researchers to expand the field to a larger set of languages. The challenges that will be discussed include multi-lingual and cross-lingual attribution, which can be particularly relevant for researchers working with underrepresented languages.

The group of authors of this proposal represents a diverse mix of geolocations (US, India, Germany), roles (academic and industrial), and career stages (Ph.D. candidates, researchers, senior researchers). While we may not necessarily represent minorities, our diverse backgrounds bring a variety of perspectives to the tutorial, enriching the content and its delivery.

11 Tutorial Information

Tutorial Type: Cutting-edge

Tutorial Venue: No preference

Tutorial Duration: 3-hour tutorial.

Reading List

1. Eliciting Attributions from LLMs with Minimal Supervision (Pasunuru et al., 2023)

2. LLM Attributor: Interactive Visual Attribution for LLM Generation (Lee et al., 2024)

3. Explaining Pre-Trained Language Models with Attribution Scores: An Analysis in Low-Resource Settings (Zhou et al., 2024)

4. Using captum to explain generative language models (Miglani et al., 2023)

5. Source-Aware Training Enables Knowledge Attribution in Language Models (Khalifa et al., 2024)

6. On the Limitations of Large Language Models (LLMs): False Attribution (Adewumi et al., 2024)

7. Attributed Question Answering: Evaluation and Modeling for Attributed Large Language Models (Bohnet et al., 2023)

8. A Survey of Large Language Models Attribution **[Recommended for preparation before joining the tutorial]** (Li et al., 2023)

9. Automatic Evaluation of Attribution by Large Language Models (Yue et al., 2023)

10. Span Level Attribution: Attribute not just sentences but spans (we just published it and I think it is a new way of defining attribution) Paper:- Peering into the Mind of Language Models: An Approach for Attribution in Contextual Question Answering (Phukan et al., 2024)

Sharing of Tutorial Materials: All the tutorial resources will be made publicly available.

12 Ethics Statement

The ethical considerations surrounding the use of LLMs and attribution methods are multifaceted. As we continue to rely on these models for tasks like document summarization, question answering, and information extraction, we must ensure the following criteria:

- **AI trustworthiness** Attribution methods aim to enhance the trustworthiness and interpretability of LLMs by substantiating the model's claims with evidence in the form of references or citations.

- **Transparency and Accountability** As the use of AI and machine learning models grows, so does the need for transparency and accountability. Attribution methods can help achieve these objectives by indicating what information has been considered.

- **Inclusivity** Dealing with multi- or cross-lingual sources presents challenges. It's important to ensure that attribution methods are inclusive and considerate of all languages and cultures.

13 Presenters

Vipula Rawte is a Machine Learning Engineer working at Adobe Experience Cloud. She is a recent Ph.D. graduate from the AI Institute, University of South Carolina, USA, advised by Dr. Amit Sheth. Her primary research interests are in Generative AI and Large Language Models. She has published and given tutorials at EMNLP, LREC-COLING, COLING, and TKDD. She has previously interned at IBM Research Zürich Lab, Dataminr, NYC, and Adobe Research, SJ. Her email is vrawte@adobe.com.

Koustava Goswami is a Senior Research Scientist at the Natural Language Processing Group (NLP) at Adobe Research, India. He graduated with a PhD in Computer Science from the National University of Ireland, Galway (now known as University of Galway, Ireland). He has published 30+ papers in NLP, Multimodal Deep Learning, and AI conferences (ACL, EMNLP, EACL, COLING, AAAI, NAACL, ICCV, ECCV, WACV, IEEE Big Data Conference, Frontier Journal, etc.). He also worked as Senior Data Scientist at an MNC and as a visiting researcher at Huawei Research, Bosch Research, etc. He is serving as a PC member at the ACL Rolling Review Paper Submission Process. He was the Organiser PC chair for the AACL-IJCNLP 2023. He is one of the organizers of the workshop SIGTYP happens every year at different NLP conference venues including ACL, EACL, and NAACL. His email is koustavag@adobe.com.

Puneet Mathur is a Research Scientist at Adobe. He graduated with a Ph.D. in Computer Science from the University of Maryland, College Park. He has published 35+ research papers on NLP, Multimodal Deep Learning, Computer Vision, Speech, and Artificial Intelligence in top-tier conferences (ACM Multimedia, ACL, NAACL, EMNLP, COLM, CVPR, AAAI, Interspeech, ICASSP, ICWSM, ACM Multimedia, and WACV). He has also worked as a quantitative analyst at a leading hedge fund and as a researcher at Meta (Facebook AI), Microsoft Research, Adobe Research, Verisk AI, and Dataminr. He also served as a senior Program Committee member of AAAI 2023, 2024, and has been the PC Chair for previous Muffin workshops organized at AAAI 2023 and IJACI 2023. His email is puneetm@adobe.com.

Nedim Lipka is a Senior Research Scientist at the Document Intelligence Lab of Adobe Research. He has a passion for research in the field of Natural Language Understanding, particularly its applications in conversational services and AI assistants. His research in the field has been published at several international conferences, including COLING, ACL, EMNLP, ICDM, WWW, CIKM, SIGIR, ECIR, etc. In addition to his research, he frequently serves as an area chair in NLP and IR conferences, further demonstrating his commitment and expertise in these areas. Most recently, he has been working on attribution for Adobe's AI assistants. His email is lipka@adobe.com.

References

Tosin Adewumi, Nudrat Habib, Lama Alkhaled, and Elisa Barney. 2024. On the limitations of large language models (llms): False attribution. *Preprint*, arXiv:2404.04631.

Bernd Bohnet, Vinh Q. Tran, Pat Verga, Roee Aharoni, Daniel Andor, Livio Baldini Soares, Massimiliano Ciaramita, Jacob Eisenstein, Kuzman Ganchev, Jonathan Herzig, Kai Hui, Tom Kwiatkowski, Ji Ma, Jianmo Ni, Lierni Sestorain Saralegui, Tal Schuster, William W. Cohen, Michael Collins, Dipanjan Das, Donald Metzler, Slav Petrov, and Kellie Webster. 2023. Attributed question answering: Evaluation and modeling for attributed large language models. *Preprint*, arXiv:2212.08037.

Siqing Huo, Negar Arabzadeh, and Charles Clarke. 2023. Retrieving supporting evidence for generative question answering. In *Proceedings of the Annual International ACM SIGIR Conference on Research and Development in Information Retrieval in the Asia Pacific Region*, pages 11–20.

Muhammad Khalifa, David Wadden, Emma Strubell, Honglak Lee, Lu Wang, Iz Beltagy, and Hao Peng. 2024. Source-aware training enables knowledge attribution in language models. *Preprint*, arXiv:2404.01019.

Seongmin Lee, Zijie J. Wang, Aishwarya Chakravarthy, Alec Helbling, ShengYun Peng, Mansi Phute, Duen Horng Chau, and Minsuk Kahng. 2024. Llm attributor: Interactive visual attribution for llm generation. *Preprint*, arXiv:2404.01361.

Dongfang Li, Zetian Sun, Xinshuo Hu, Zhenyu Liu, Ziyang Chen, Baotian Hu, Aiguo Wu, and Min Zhang. 2023. A survey of large language models attribution. *Preprint*, arXiv:2311.03731.

Vivek Miglani, Aobo Yang, Aram H Markosyan, Diego Garcia-Olano, and Narine Kokhlikyan. 2023. Using captum to explain generative language models. *arXiv preprint arXiv:2312.05491*.

Ramakanth Pasunuru, Koustuv Sinha, Armen Aghajanyan, LILI YU, Tianlu Wang, Daniel M Bikel, Luke Zettlemoyer, Maryam Fazel-Zarandi, and Asli Celikyilmaz. 2023. Eliciting attributions from llms with minimal supervision.

Anirudh Phukan, Shwetha Somasundaram, Apoorv Saxena, Koustava Goswami, and Balaji Vasan Srinivasan. 2024. Peering into the mind of language models: An approach for attribution in contextual question answering. *CoRR*, abs/2405.17980.

Yuan Sui, Jiaru Zou, Mengyu Zhou, Xinyi He, Lun Du, Shi Han, and Dongmei Zhang. 2023. Tap4llm: Table provider on sampling, augmenting, and packing semi-structured data for large language model reasoning. *ArXiv*, abs/2312.09039.

Xiang Yue, Boshi Wang, Ziru Chen, Kai Zhang, Yu Su, and Huan Sun. 2023. Automatic evaluation of attribution by large language models. In *Findings of the Association for Computational Linguistics: EMNLP 2023*, pages 4615–4635, Singapore. Association for Computational Linguistics.

Wei Zhou, Heike Adel, Hendrik Schuff, and Ngoc Thang Vu. 2024. Explaining pre-trained language models with attribution scores: An analysis in low-resource settings. *arXiv preprint arXiv:2403.05338*.

IJCNLP Tutorial - Continual Learning in Large Language Models : Foundations to Frontiers

P.K. Srijith
IIT Hyderabad, India

Shrey Satapara
Fujitsu Research, India

Sarath Chandar
Ecole Polytechnique de Montreal
Mila, Quebec AI Institute, Canada

1 Title

Continual Learning in Large Language Models : Foundations to Frontiers

2 Abstract

Continual learning (CL) provides deep learning models the ability to learn a sequence of tasks under resource constraint settings, without forgetting previously acquired knowledge. This is particularly useful for multilingual NLP for low-resource languages, where incremental data collection is common and the compute cost is crucial. This tutorial will introduce key CL methodologies and their applications in natural language processing (NLP), covering both foundational techniques and modern challenges posed by large language models (LLMs). This tutorial covers foundational CL strategies based on regularization, replay, and network architecture. We explore NLP-specific CL scenarios such as task-incremental, language-incremental, and joint task-language incremental setups, along with methodologies to address them. A major emphasize of the tutorial is on continual learning for large language models (LLMs), examining challenges in applying CL for LLMs and the benefits it can provide in LLM training and inference. We further explore the connection between several advances in LLM such as model merging and continual learning. This tutorial is suitable for NLP researchers, practitioners, and students interested in lifelong learning, multilingual NLP, or large language models. It is designed as a half-day tutorial at IJCNLP 2025 and fall under the category of Introduction to Non-CL/Non-NLP Topic.

Proceedings of the 14th International Joint Conference on Natural Language Processing and the 4th Conference of the Asia-Pacific Chapter of the Association for Computational Linguistics: Tutorial Abstract, pages 6–17
December 20-24, 2025 ©2025 Association for Computational Linguistics

3 Introduction

Natural language processing models require periodic updates to address challenges such as shifts in data distribution or adaptation to new domains or tasks [3]. In real-world applications, the ability to learn new tasks or languages is essential to maintain the relevance and effectiveness of such systems. For instance, a customer service system initially designed to handle tasks like order tracking and returns in English may need to expand its capabilities to support additional languages or address new functions such as resolving payment-related issues.

Adapting the model to new data or tasks can affect its ability to retain previously learned tasks or languages — a phenomenon known as catastrophic forgetting [10]. Continual learning (CL) or lifelong learning is proposed to address the challenges in adapting a pre-trained language model (PLM) to a new task, language or domain while retaining previously obtained knowledge [7, 18, 3, 25, 34]. It is an active research area in Artificial Intelligence and is extremely useful to address several problems in NLP. There has been a growing interest in the research community in using CL methods to adapt NLP models across several tasks and languages. In recent years, large language models (LLMs) have made significant strides in addressing a wide range of NLP tasks. CL methods were found to be helpful at various stages of the LLM tarining and inference [40]. Moreover, several common practices followed by LLM practitioners such as model merging [41] can be grounded to the CL methodology and philosophy.

IJCNLP–AACL has a strong focus on multilingual NLP and under-resourced languages in Asia and beyond. Incremental data collection across languages is a common norm for NLP tasks in low-resource languages. The continual learning strategies are best suited for such scenarios where we want to adapt the capability of NLP models to new languages, domains and tasks without affecting its existing capabilities. Further. CL approaches provide parameter-efficient and data efficient learning process, leading to low compute and data requirements. This further emphasize the importance of CL for NLP models especially in developing countries, where the expense of computation poses a significant constraint.

In this tutorial, our main objective is to introduce and discuss continual learning methods in NLP and in particular, for large language models. The Tutorial will start with the foundations of continual learning, including several techniques devised to mitigate catastrophic forgetting. Then, it will focus on the application of CL for NLP tasks, including learning across multiple languages. The final but also the major emphasize of the tutorial will be on continual learning for LLMs and underlying challenges and opportunities in this direction. We also discuss the connections between CL and several emerging practices in LLMs, bridging the conceptual framework of continual learning and advances in large language models.

4 Target Audience

This tutorial is aimed at the following audience.

- NLP researchers and graduate students exploring lifelong learning models.
- Practitioners working on multilingual and multi-task systems.
- Developers of LLM-based applications needing continual adaptation.

Prerequisites:

- Basic familiarity with deep learning and NLP models (e.g., transformers).
- Exposure to supervised learning and NLP tasks.
- Python programming skills (for optional code follow-along or resources).

Expected Participants : 150

5 Outline

The tutorial provides a comprehensive coverage of continual learning and its efficacy in Natural Language Processing. We start with a basic introduction to continual learning, covering various CL techniques such as replay, regularization, parameter isolation and growth based techniques [37]. Following this, we discuss CL techniques applied for the NLP problems, covering various scenarios such as task incremental learning, language incremental learning, and joint task-language incremental learning [32]. Considering that the latest advances in NLP is achieved through LLMs, a major portion of the tutorial is devoted to CL in LLMs. We discuss the LLM-specific CL strategies such as continual pre-training (CPT), continual instruction tuning (CIT), and continual alignment (CA) [40]. We bring connections between CL and other popular techniques in LLMs such as model merging and retrieval augmented generation (RAG). We further discuss other opportunities in this topic, such as continual learning over LLM agents. We expect the tutorial to be half-day, approximately 3.5 hours including 30 min break. A brief outline of the talk is provided below, and a detailed plan is provided in the following subsections.

1. Continual Learning Basics (45 min)
2. Continual Learning in NLP (45 min)
3. Continual Learning in LLMs (90 min)

5.1 Continual Learning Basics (45 Min)

In the first part of the tutorial, we discuss the fundamentals of CL, introducing concepts such as catastrophic forgetting [10], and several scenarios of CL such as task incremental learning, domain incremental learning and class incremental learning [7]. Then, we provide an overview of techniques developed to provide CL capability in deep learning models.

Continual learning (CL) approaches are broadly categorized into three main paradigms: Regularization-based methods aim to reduce forgetting by incorporating additional regularization terms in the loss function while learning new tasks [7]. These terms constrain changes to model parameters, minimizing interference with previously learned tasks. For example, Elastic Weight Consolidation (EWC) penalizes updates to important parameters based on task-specific importance scores [20]. Alternatively, some approaches apply functional regularization, preserving the model's behavior on prior tasks through distillation losses between old and updated models [23]. In this context, we also discuss the CL approaches developed based on hypernetworks [14, 36, 5].

We explore architecture-based methods, which avoid interference by allocating distinct sets of parameters for each task. This can involve using separate models, partitioning a single model into task-specific subnetworks [24], or progressively expanding the architecture with additional neurons to accommodate new tasks [43]. We also examine the parameter-efficient Adapter based techniques which were found to be effective for CL in pre-trained large models [8, 11, 1]. Finally, we consider Replay-based methods, which use selective storage and reuse of historical data during continual learning. A small buffer retains representative samples from past tasks, which are replayed when learning new tasks to approximate earlier data distributions [31, 30]. Variants of this approach differ primarily in how samples are selected and managed within the buffer. Some methods forego explicit storage by employing generative models trained to reproduce data from previous tasks [33].

5.2 Continual Learning in NLP (45 Min)

Continual learning in NLP involves learning across new tasks, new languages, or across both tasks and languages, each giving rise to a different incremental learning setup. Generally, it is categorized into task-incremental continual learning (TICL) and language-incremental continual learning (LICL) [4]. Existing works in NLP address these settings through the already discussed CL techniques such as those based on Replay, Regularization and Architecture. We also discuss data sets, and evaluation metrics used to perform CL for the NLP tasks.

Task-Incremental Continual Learning (TICL) : TICL [7] focuses on algorithms that can learn from non-stationary task sequences while retaining knowledge of prior tasks. LAMOL [35] adopts a pseudo-replay strategy, jointly learning downstream tasks and generating synthetic training data for them. Parameter isolation techniques, such as [38], maintain a frozen pretrained model while learning compact task-specific parameters, whereas [19] train distinct adapter modules for each task. To perform CL in language models, Progressive Prompts [29] introduce new soft prompts for every task and append them sequentially to those learned earlier.

Language-Incremental Continual Learning (LICL) : LICL [26] investigates continual learning in multilingual contexts. A significant portion of the work targets neural machine translation (NMT) based tasks. Approaches such as [2, 6, 13, 9] replace a shared vocabulary with compact, language-specific vocabularies, followed by fine-tuning the corresponding embeddings on new-language parallel corpora. [6] applies knowledge distillation to preserve performance during LICL, while [26] examines it through the lens of knowledge retention and cross-lingual generalization. A more general scenario of incremental learning across both tasks and languages was considered in [32], where they propose a flexible adapter-based continual learning algorithm.

5.3 Continual Learning in LLMs (90 Min)

CL in the context of LLMs introduces new challenges and opportunities due to the scale, complexity, and general-purpose nature of these models. CL can be incorporated in LLMs at various stages like pretraining, fine-tuning and alignment. Pretraining LLMs on evolving corpus such as new web data, code or scientific literature is a natural setup for CL. In the continual pre-Training (CPT), notable works such as TiC-LM [22], lifelong pretraining (Lifelong LLMs), and TemporalWiki [15] explore evolving corpora over time, while methods like D-CPT [28], the CMR Scaling Law [12], and Mix-CPT [17] provide principled control over data mixture, domain adaptation, and format alignment.

In the finetuning stage, LLMs are adatpted to new tasks, user specific data or senarios through instruction tuning. In Continual Fine-Tuning (CFT), we cover methods like PCL [42] (prompt-based continual learning), SPARC [16] (subspace-aware prompt adaptation), Optimal Brain Iterative Merging [39] (OBIM for mitigating interference), and LFPT5 [27] (prompt-tuned lifelong few-shot learning) to address the challenges of retaining prior capabilities while adapting to new tasks. The alignment stage can benefit from CL, as human preferences evolve or new safety concerns arises, the model needs to adapt to responses without undermining prior alignment efforts. There are some prominent works like CoPR [44] (Continual Preference via Optimal Policy Regularization), and CPPO [45] (Continual PPO for RLHF-style updates) explores CL at the alignment stage.

Continual learning in LLMs open up several opportunities and possibilities in adapting LLM to specific languages and tasks, especially in low-resource language domains. It allows the LLM model to continually adapt to new languages without losing its general capabilities, and without retraining from scratch. This is important in the LLM context due to the computational cost in retraining the LLM, and the unavailability of data on which LLMs are trained. We also discuss connections between continual learning and some practices in the LLM community, such as retrieval augmented generation (RAG) [21] and model merging [41, 46]. We also discuss future possibilities and avenues in applying CL in LLMs, for instance, in the context of LLM agents.

6 Diversity Considerations

- The topic supports language diversity by addressing continual adaptation to multilingual inputs.
- Encourages inclusion of low-resource languages and domains, promoting fairness in model development.
- The tutorial's content is especially valuable for researchers from under-represented regions (e.g., South/Southeast Asia, Africa, Eastern Europe) where multilingual adaptation is vital and compute cost is crucial.

7 Reading List

7.1 Introductory Papers for Continual Learning

- French, R. M. Catastrophic forgetting in connectionist networks: Can it be predicted? Proceedings of the 15th Annual Cognitive Science Society Conference, 103–108, 1993.
- Liu, B. Lifelong machine learning: a paradigm for continuous learning. Proceedings of Frontiers of Computer Science, 11(3), 359–361, 2017.
- Kirkpatrick, J., Pascanu, R., Rabinowitz, N., Veness, J., Desjardins, G., Rusu, A. A., Milan, K., Quan, J., Ramalho, T., Grabska-Barwinska, A., & others. Overcoming catastrophic forgetting in neural networks. Proceedings of the National Academy of Sciences, 114(13), 3521–3526, 2017.

7.2 Surveys on Continual Learning

- Wang, L., Zhang, X., Su, H., & Zhu, J. A Comprehensive Survey of Continual Learning: Theory, Method and Application. Arxiv, 2024.
- M. Biesialska, K. Biesialska, and M. R. Costa-juss'a. Continual lifelong learning in natural language processing: A survey, Proceedings of the 28th International Conference on Computational Linguistics, pages 6523–6541, Barcelona, Spain, Dec. 2020.
- M. De Lange, R. Aljundi, M. Masana, S. Parisot, X. Jia, A. Leonardis, G. Slabaugh, and T. Tuytelaars. A continual learning survey: Defying forgetting in classification tasks. IEEE transactions on pattern analysis and machine intelligence, 44(7):3366–3385, 2021.

More papers related to continual learning can be found at ContinualAI Github Repository[1]

8 Presenters

Sarath Chandar, Canada CIFAR AI Chair, Associate Professor, Department of Computer and Software Engineering, École Polytechnique de Montréal. Sarath Chandar is an Associate Professor at Polytechnique Montreal where he leads the Chandar Research Lab. He is also a core faculty member at Mila, the Quebec AI Institute. Sarath holds a Canada CIFAR AI Chair and the Canada Research Chair in Lifelong Machine Learning. His research interests include continual/lifelong learning, deep learning, optimization, reinforcement learning, natural language processing and AI for science. To promote research in lifelong learning, Sarath created the Conference on Lifelong Learning Agents (CoLLAs) in 2022 and served as a program chair for 2022 and 2023. He regularly gives tutorials and talks on continual learning at international venues and summer schools. He received his Ph.D. from the University of Montreal. Webpage: (http://sarathchandar.in/).

P . K. Srijith, Associate Professor, Department of Computer Science and Engineering, IIT Hyderabad, India. P. K. Srijith is an Associate Professor at the Department of Computer Science and Engineering, IIT Hyderabad and is also associated with the Department of Artificial Intelligence, IIT Hyderabad. He is interested in developing learning algorithms such as continual learning, causal learning, Bayesian learning, multi-modal learning for vision and natural language processing problems. He has recently published several papers on continual learning for both vision and NLP, and has offered talks on continual learning at workshops and courses on CL at IIT Hyderabad. He has organized international conferences and several workshops. He was the organizing chair for the Asian Conference for Machine Learning (ACML 2022) at Hyderabad and in the senior program committee for the past few years. He recently co-organized the Continual Causal Bridge program at AAAI 2025 in Philadelphia, U.S.A. He has won awards such as the Sony Research Award 2021 for his research on continual learning. He received his Ph.D. from Indian Institute of Science (IISc.), Bangalore and did his postdoctoral research on NLP at University of Sheffield and University of Melbourne. More details on his research can be found at his website (https://sites.google.com/site/pksrijith/home) and the lab website (https://sites.google.com/view/brainiith/home).

Shrey Satapara, Researcher - II, AI Lab, Fujitsu Research, India. Shrey is an early-career researcher currently working as a Researcher-II at Fujitsu Research of India in the Agentic Science team, where he focuses on multi-agent systems and LLM-based workflows. His research spans continual learning, multilingual NLP, and machine translation, with several peer-reviewed publications. Over the past four years, he has co-organized shared tasks in hate speech detection in indo aryan languages and Indian language summarization.

[1]https://github.com/ContinualAI/continual-learning-papers

He also has experience conducting tutorials as a teaching assistant in ML and NLP during his postgraduate studies. He received Master's Degree in Artificial Intelligence from IIT Hyderabad. Homepage: (https://shreysatapara.github.io)

9 Other Information

We expect the number of participants to be atleast 100. The estimated count is based on the number of participants registered for the continual learning workshop organized at the Asian Conference on Machine Learning 2022 held in Hyderabad, India. However, with the recent popularity of continual learning and large language models, we expect the number to be around 150.

Logistical Requirements: We will be presenting using a powerpoint/PDF slides and online demos on our laptops, no other special requirements are needed except good internet connectivity.

10 Ethics Statement

There are no ethical concerns regarding the proposed topic.

11 Relevent List of Papers:

1. M. Biesialska, K. Biesialska, and M. R. Costa-juss'a. Continual lifelong learning in natural language processing: A survey, Proceedings of the 28th International Conference on Computational Linguistics, pages 6523–6541, Barcelona, Spain, Dec. 2020.

2. M. De Lange, R. Aljundi, M. Masana, S. Parisot, X. Jia, A. Leonardis, G. Slabaugh, and T. Tuytelaars. A continual learning survey: Defying forgetting in classification tasks. IEEE transactions on pattern analysis and machine intelligence, 44(7):3366–3385, 2021.

3. S. Satapara and P. K. Srijith. TL-CL: Task and language incremental continual learning. In Proceedings of the 2024 Conference on Empirical Methods in Natural Language Processing, Association for Computational Linguistics, pages 12123–12142, Miami, Florida, USA, Nov. 2024.

4. T. Wu, L. Luo, Y. Li, S. Pan, T. Vu, and G. Haffari. Continual learning for large language models: A survey. arXiv preprint arXiv:2402.01364, 2024.

References

[1] S. Adhikari, D. S. Chandra, P. K. Srijith, P. Wasnik, and N. Oneo. Adaprefix++: Integrating adapters prefixes and hypernetwork for continual learn-

ing. In *Proceedings of the Winter Conference on Applications of Computer Vision (WACV)*, pages 7298–7307, February 2025.

[2] A. Berard. Continual learning in multilingual NMT via language-specific embeddings. In L. Barrault, O. Bojar, F. Bougares, R. Chatterjee, M. R. Costa-jussa, C. Federmann, M. Fishel, A. Fraser, M. Freitag, Y. Graham, R. Grundkiewicz, P. Guzman, B. Haddow, M. Huck, A. J. Yepes, P. Koehn, T. Kocmi, A. Martins, M. Morishita, and C. Monz, editors, *Proceedings of the Sixth Conference on Machine Translation*, pages 542–565, Online, Nov. 2021. Association for Computational Linguistics.

[3] M. Biesialska, K. Biesialska, and M. R. Costa-jussà. Continual lifelong learning in natural language processing: A survey. In D. Scott, N. Bel, and C. Zong, editors, *Proceedings of the 28th International Conference on Computational Linguistics*, pages 6523–6541, Barcelona, Spain (Online), Dec. 2020. International Committee on Computational Linguistics.

[4] M. Biesialska, K. Biesialska, and M. R. Costa-jussà. Continual lifelong learning in natural language processing: A survey. In D. Scott, N. Bel, and C. Zong, editors, *Proceedings of the 28th International Conference on Computational Linguistics*, pages 6523–6541, Barcelona, Spain (Online), Dec. 2020. International Committee on Computational Linguistics.

[5] D. S. Chandra, S. Varshney, P. K. Srijith, and S. Gupta. Continual learning with dependency preserving hypernetworks. In *Proceedings of the IEEE/CVF Winter Conference on Applications of Computer Vision (WACV)*, pages 2339–2348, January 2023.

[6] Y.-S. Chuang, S.-Y. Su, and Y.-N. Chen. Lifelong language knowledge distillation. In B. Webber, T. Cohn, Y. He, and Y. Liu, editors, *Proceedings of the 2020 Conference on Empirical Methods in Natural Language Processing (EMNLP)*, pages 2914–2924, Online, Nov. 2020. Association for Computational Linguistics.

[7] M. De Lange, R. Aljundi, M. Masana, S. Parisot, X. Jia, A. Leonardis, G. Slabaugh, and T. Tuytelaars. A continual learning survey: Defying forgetting in classification tasks. *IEEE transactions on pattern analysis and machine intelligence*, 44(7):3366–3385, 2021.

[8] B. Ermiş, G. Zappella, M. Wistuba, A. Rawal, and C. Archambeau. Memory efficient continual learning with transformers. In *Advances in Neural Information Processing Systems (NeurIPS) 2022*, 2022.

[9] C. Escolano, M. R. Costa-jussà, and J. A. R. Fonollosa. From bilingual to multilingual neural machine translation by incremental training. In F. Alva-Manchego, E. Choi, and D. Khashabi, editors, *Proceedings of the 57th Annual Meeting of the Association for Computational Linguistics: Student Research Workshop*, pages 236–242, Florence, Italy, July 2019. Association for Computational Linguistics.

[10] R. M. French. Catastrophic forgetting in connectionist networks: Can it be predicted? In *Proceedings of the 15th Annual Cognitive Science Society Conference*, pages 103–108, 1993.

[11] Q. Gao, C. Zhao, Y. Sun, T. Xi, G. Zhang, B. Ghanem, and J. Zhang. A unified continual learning framework with general parameter-efficient tuning. In *Proceedings of the IEEE/CVF International Conference on Computer Vision (ICCV)*, pages 11483–11493, 2023.

[12] J. Gu, Z. Yang, C. Ding, R. Zhao, and F. Tan. Cmr scaling law: Predicting critical mixture ratios for continual pre-training of language models, 2024.

[13] S. Gu, B. Hu, and Y. Feng. Continual learning of neural machine translation within low forgetting risk regions. In Y. Goldberg, Z. Kozareva, and Y. Zhang, editors, *Proceedings of the 2022 Conference on Empirical Methods in Natural Language Processing*, pages 1707–1718, Abu Dhabi, United Arab Emirates, Dec. 2022. Association for Computational Linguistics.

[14] D. Ha, A. M. Dai, and Q. V. Le. Hypernetworks. In *International Conference on Learning Representations*, 2017.

[15] J. Jang, S. Ye, C. Lee, S. Yang, J. Shin, J. Han, G. Kim, and M. Seo. Temporalwiki: A lifelong benchmark for training and evaluating ever-evolving language models. In *In Proceddings of EMNLP*, 2022.

[16] D. Jayasuriya, S. Tayebati, D. Ettori, R. Krishnan, and A. R. Trivedi. Sparc: Subspace-aware prompt adaptation for robust continual learning in llms, 2025.

[17] J. Jiang, J. Li, X. Zhao, Y. Song, T. Zhang, and J.-R. Wen. Mix-cpt: A domain adaptation framework via decoupling knowledge learning and format alignment. In Y. Yue, A. Garg, N. Peng, F. Sha, and R. Yu, editors, *International Conference on Representation Learning*, volume 2025, pages 82198–82216, 2025.

[18] Z. Ke and B. Liu. Continual learning of natural language processing tasks: A survey. *arXiv preprint arXiv:2211.12701*, 2022.

[19] S. Khan, S. Agarwal, and P. Srijith. Lifelong language learning with adapter based transformers. In *Continual Lifelong Learning Workshop at ACML 2022*, 2022.

[20] J. Kirkpatrick, R. Pascanu, N. Rabinowitz, J. Veness, G. Desjardins, A. A. Rusu, K. Milan, J. Quan, T. Ramalho, A. Grabska-Barwinska, et al. Overcoming catastrophic forgetting in neural networks. *Proceedings of the national academy of sciences*, 114(13):3521–3526, 2017.

[21] P. Lewis, E. Perez, A. Piktus, F. Petroni, V. Karpukhin, N. Goyal, H. Küttler, M. Lewis, W.-t. Yih, T. Rocktäschel, S. Riedel, and D. Kiela. Retrieval-augmented generation for knowledge-intensive nlp tasks. In *Advances in Neural Information Processing Systems*, volume 33, pages 9459–9474, 2020.

[22] J. Li, M. Armandpour, S. I. Mirzadeh, S. Mehta, V. Shankar, R. Vemulapalli, O. Tuzel, M. Farajtabar, H. Pouransari, and F. Faghri. Tic-LM: A multi-year benchmark for continual pretraining of language models. In *NeurIPS 2024 Workshop on Scalable Continual Learning for Lifelong Foundation Models*, 2024.

[23] Z. Li and D. Hoiem. Learning without forgetting. *IEEE transactions on pattern analysis and machine intelligence*, 40(12):2935–2947, 2017.

[24] A. Mallya and S. Lazebnik. Packnet: Adding multiple tasks to a single network by iterative pruning. In *2018 IEEE/CVF Conference on Computer Vision and Pattern Recognition*, pages 7765–7773, 2018.

[25] S. V. Mehta, D. Patil, S. Chandar, and E. Strubell. An empirical investigation of the role of pre-training in lifelong learning. *Journal of Machine Learning Research*, 24(214):1–50, 2023.

[26] M. M'hamdi, X. Ren, and J. May. Cross-lingual continual learning. In A. Rogers, J. Boyd-Graber, and N. Okazaki, editors, *Proceedings of the 61st Annual Meeting of the Association for Computational Linguistics (Volume 1: Long Papers)*, pages 3908–3943, Toronto, Canada, July 2023. Association for Computational Linguistics.

[27] C. Qin and S. Joty. LFPT5: A unified framework for lifelong few-shot language learning based on prompt tuning of t5. In *International Conference on Learning Representations*, 2022.

[28] H. Que, J. Liu, G. Zhang, C. Zhang, X. Qu, Y. Ma, F. Duan, Z. Bai, J. Wang, Y. Zhang, X. Tan, J. Fu, J. Wang, L. Qu, W. Su, and B. Zheng. D-cpt law: domain-specific continual pre-training scaling law for large language models. In *Proceedings of the 38th International Conference on Neural Information Processing Systems*, NIPS '24, Red Hook, NY, USA, 2025. Curran Associates Inc.

[29] A. Razdaibiedina, Y. Mao, R. Hou, M. Khabsa, M. Lewis, and A. Almahairi. Progressive prompts: Continual learning for language models. In *International Conference on Learning Representations*, 2023.

[30] M. Riemer, I. Cases, R. Ajemian, M. Liu, I. Rish, Y. Tu, and G. Tesauro. Learning to learn without forgetting by maximizing transfer and minimizing interference. In *7th International Conference on Learning Representations, ICLR 2019, New Orleans, LA, USA, May 6-9, 2019*. OpenReview.net, 2019.

[31] D. Rolnick, A. Ahuja, J. Schwarz, T. Lillicrap, and G. Wayne. Experience replay for continual learning. *Advances in neural information processing systems*, 32, 2019.

[32] S. Satapara and P. K. Srijith. TL-CL: Task and language incremental continual learning. In *Proceedings of the 2024 Conference on Empirical Methods in Natural Language Processing*, pages 12123–12142, Miami, Florida, USA, Nov. 2024. Association for Computational Linguistics.

[33] H. Shin, J. K. Lee, J. Kim, and J. Kim. Continual learning with deep generative replay. In I. Guyon, U. V. Luxburg, S. Bengio, H. Wallach, R. Fergus, S. Vishwanathan, and R. Garnett, editors, *Advances in Neural Information Processing Systems*, volume 30. Curran Associates, Inc., 2017.

[34] S. Sodhani, S. Chandar, and Y. Bengio. Toward training recurrent neural networks for lifelong learning. *Neural Comput.*, 32(1):1–35, Jan. 2020.

[35] F. Sun, C. Ho, and H. Lee. LAMAL: language modeling is all you need for lifelong language learning. *CoRR*, abs/1909.03329, 2019.

[36] J. von Oswald, C. Henning, B. F. Grewe, and J. Sacramento. Continual learning with hypernetworks. In *International Conference on Learning Representations*, 2020.

[37] L. Wang, X. Zhang, H. Su, and J. Zhu. A comprehensive survey of continual learning: Theory, method and application. *IEEE Trans. Pattern Anal. Mach. Intell.*, 46(8):5362–5383, Aug. 2024.

[38] Z. Wang, Y. Liu, T. Ji, X. Wang, Y. Wu, C. Jiang, Y. Chao, Z. Han, L. Wang, X. Shao, and W. Zeng. Rehearsal-free continual language learning via efficient parameter isolation. In A. Rogers, J. Boyd-Graber, and N. Okazaki, editors, *Proceedings of the 61st Annual Meeting of the Association for Computational Linguistics (Volume 1: Long Papers)*, pages 10933–10946, Toronto, Canada, July 2023. Association for Computational Linguistics.

[39] Z. Wang, Z. Mao, Y. Qiao, Y. Wu, and B. Li. Optimal brain iterative merging: Mitigating interference in LLM merging. *CoRR*, abs/2502.12217, 2025.

[40] T. Wu, L. Luo, Y. Li, S. Pan, T. Vu, and G. Haffari. Continual learning for large language models: A survey. *arXiv preprint arXiv:2402.01364*, 2024.

[41] E. Yang, L. Shen, G. Guo, X. Wang, X. Cao, J. Zhang, and D. Tao. Model merging in llms, mllms, and beyond: Methods, theories, applications and opportunities. *arXiv preprint arXiv:2408.07666*, 2024.

[42] M. Yang, F. Yang, Y. Guo, S. Xu, T. Zhou, Y. Chen, S. Shao, J. Liu, and Y. Gao. Pcl: Prompt-based continual learning for user modeling in recommender systems. In *Companion Proceedings of the ACM on Web Conference 2025*, page 1475–1479. ACM, May 2025.

[43] J. Yoon, E. Yang, J. Lee, and S. J. Hwang. Lifelong learning with dynamically expandable networks. In *International Conference on Learning Representations*, 2018.

[44] H. Zhang, L. Gui, Y. Lei, Y. Zhai, Y. Zhang, Z. Zhang, Y. He, H. Wang, Y. Yu, K.-F. Wong, B. Liang, and R. Xu. COPR: Continual human preference learning via optimal policy regularization. In *Findings of the Association for Computational Linguistics: ACL 2025*, pages 5377–5398, Vienna, Austria, 2025. Association for Computational Linguistics.

[45] H. Zhang, Y. Lei, L. Gui, M. Yang, Y. He, H. Wang, and R. Xu. CPPO: Continual learning for reinforcement learning with human feedback. In *The Twelfth International Conference on Learning Representations*, 2024.

[46] Y. Zhou, L. Song, B. Wang, and W. Chen. MetaGPT: Merging large language models using model exclusive task arithmetic. In Y. Al-Onaizan, M. Bansal, and Y.-N. Chen, editors, *Proceedings of the 2024 Conference on Empirical Methods in Natural Language Processing*, pages 1711–1724, Miami, Florida, USA, Nov. 2024. Association for Computational Linguistics.

AACL-2025 Tutorial Title:

NLP for Affective Science:
Exploring Fundamental Questions on Emotions through Language and Computation

Speakers:

Dr. Krishnapriya Vishnubhotla (she/her)
Research Associate, National Research Council Canada

Dr. Saif M. Mohammad (he, him)
Principal Research Scientist, National Research Council Canada

Abstract: Affect refers to the fundamental neural processes that generate and regulate emotions, moods, and feeling states. Affect and emotions are central to how we organize meaning, to our behaviour, to our health and well-being, and to our very survival. Despite this, and even though most of us are all intimately familiar with emotions in everyday life, there is much we do not know about how emotions work, and how they impact our lives. **Affective Science** is a broad interdisciplinary field that explores these and other related questions about affect and emotions.

Since **language** is a powerful mechanism of emotion expression, there is great potential in using language data and computation to shed light on fundamental questions about emotions. However, even though much progress has been made in areas such as sentiment analysis and affective computing, much of the research focus is squarely on automatically classifying pieces of text. In this tutorial, we will present an introduction to Affective Science and argue that NLP is uniquely positioned to contribute to it: to boldly explore a new frontier — to use language and computation to ask fundamental questions about how emotions and affect work. We will cover the broad areas of research within this nascent field of study - **Computational Affective Science (CAS)**:

1. The Theories and Nature of Affect
2. The Relationship of Affect with the Mind, Body, and the World Around Us
3. Affective Data and Resources
4. Affective Tasks and Methods (including Generative AI)
5. Applications
6. Ethics, Fairness, Theory Integration, Philosophical Implications

And discuss specific case studies and key pieces of work within CAS on emotion dynamics, emotion granularity, affect lexicons, stereotype cognition models, and the language of interoception.

This tutorial is a vision of Computational Affective Science that advances our understanding of emotion and human experience, builds useful applications, and plays an active role in navigating the societal implications of the powerful underlying technologies.

Bios:

Dr. Krishnapriya Vishnubhotla is a Research Associate at the National Research Council Canada (NRC). She received her PhD in Computer Science from the University of Toronto in 2024. Her thesis projects focused on modelling variation in language use as a function of

Proceedings of the 14th International Joint Conference on Natural Language Processing and the 4th Conference of the Asia-Pacific Chapter of the Association for Computational Linguistics: Tutorial Abstract, pages 18–19
December 20-24, 2025 ©2025 Association for Computational Linguistics

speaker identity, a research area that falls at the intersection of natural language processing, sociolinguistics, and affective science. She is interested in leveraging large text datasets to better understand how facets of individual identity and communicative goals affect the ways in which information is conveyed via language, and more broadly in the applications of NLP technologies in the social sciences and humanities.

Photo:

Dr. Saif M. Mohammad is a Principal Research Scientist at the National Research Council Canada (NRC). He received his Ph.D. in Computer Science from the University of Toronto. Before joining NRC, he was a Research Associate at the Institute of Advanced Computer Studies at the University of Maryland, College Park. His research interests are in Natural Language Processing (NLP), especially Lexical Semantics, Computational Affective Science, AI Ethics, and Computational Social Science. He is currently an associate editor for Computational Linguistics and TACL, and Senior Area Chair for ACL Rolling Review. His word--emotion resources, such as the NRC Emotion Lexicon and VAD Lexicon, are widely used for analyzing emotions in text. His work has garnered significant media attention, including articles in Time, SlashDot, LiveScience, io9, The Physics arXiv Blog, PC World, and Popular Science.
Webpage: http://saifmohammad.com

Photo:

Human-Agent Teaming for Higher-Order Thinking Augmentation

Chung-Chi Chen
Artificial Intelligence Research Center,
National Institute of Advanced Industrial Science and Technology, Japan
c.c.chen@acm.org

Abstract

Human-agent teaming refers to humans and artificial agents working together toward shared goals, and recent advances in artificial intelligence, including large language models and autonomous robots, have intensified interest in using these agents not only for automation but also to augment higher-order cognition. Higher-order thinking involves complex mental processes such as critical thinking, creative problem solving, abstract reasoning, and metacognition, and intelligent agents hold the potential to act as genuine teammates that complement human strengths and address cognitive limitations. This tutorial[1] synthesizes emerging research on human-agent teaming for cognitive augmentation by outlining the foundations of higher-order thinking and the psychological frameworks that describe it, reviewing key concepts and interaction paradigms in human–AI collaboration, and examining applications across education, healthcare, military decision-making, scientific discovery, and creative industries, where systems such as language models, decision-support tools, multi-agent architectures, explainable AI, and hybrid human–AI methods are used to support complex reasoning and expert judgment. It also discusses the major challenges involved in achieving meaningful augmentation, including the calibration of trust, the need for transparency, the development of shared mental models, the role of human adaptability and training, and broader ethical concerns. The tutorial further identifies gaps such as limited evidence of long-term improvement in human cognitive abilities and insufficient co-adaptation between humans and agents. Finally, it outlines future directions involving real-time cognitive alignment, long-term studies of cognitive development, co-adaptive learning systems, ethics-aware AI teammates, and new benchmarks for evaluating collaborative cognition, offering a comprehensive overview of current progress and a roadmap for advancing human-agent teaming as a means of enhancing higher-order human thinking.

[1]https://nlpfin.github.io/sites/aacl2025.html

1 Human-Agent Teaming

Traditional AI or automation has often been viewed as a tool that a human uses – a passive instrument executing tasks under human direction. In contrast, human-agent teaming (HAT) envisions AI systems as active team members that collaborate with humans in a more symmetric, interdependent manner. In a HAT scenario, the human and AI share a common goal, and each contributes their distinct capabilities to jointly achieve outcomes that neither could alone as effectively. HAT is sometimes termed human–AI teaming (HAIT), human–autonomy teaming, or human–AI collaboration – reflecting overlapping concepts. Across these definitions, the emphasis is on leveraging the complementary strengths of humans (e.g. intuition, ethical judgment, creativity) and AI agents (e.g. speed, data processing, precision) in an integrated way. For example, an AI might generate options or analyze large datasets while the human makes contextual judgments and provides oversight, together making a better decision than either could alone. Crucially, HAT is seen as a human-centered approach to AI deployment: its aim is not just raw efficiency, but also to ensure human well-being, learning, and motivation by making the AI a supportive partner rather than a black-box replacer.

As AI technologies become more autonomous and "smart," people begin to perceive them as social agents rather than mere devices. This opens the door to designing AI that engages in teamwork behaviors – communicating, adapting, even exhibiting social qualities like encouragement or etiquette – thereby fitting more naturally into human teams. Make an AI feel like a teammate instead of a tool, including the agent's agency (ability to act independently), benevolence (being oriented to help the

Proceedings of the 14th International Joint Conference on Natural Language Processing and the 4th Conference of the Asia-Pacific Chapter of the Association for Computational Linguistics: Tutorial Abstract, pages 20–24
December 20-24, 2025 ©2025 Association for Computational Linguistics

human), communicativeness, interdependence (its actions depend on human actions and vice versa), synchrony (coordination and timing in interaction), and a team focus (shared goals). When humans perceive these attributes in an AI – for instance, an AI that proactively updates a plan in response to a human's change in strategy (showing interdependence and initiative) – they are more likely to trust and "team up" with it rather than treat it as just an automated tool (Lyons et al., 2021).

An important aspect of HAT is the level of autonomy the agent has. Early framework (Sheridan and Parasuraman, 2005) defined levels ranging from complete human control to full machine control. In HAT contexts, instead of replacing the human at high autonomy, the goal is a balance where the AI has enough autonomy to act proactively as a teammate, but not so much that the human is out of the loop. Lyons et al. (2021) suggest that to qualify as a "teammate," an agent must possess a degree of autonomy (to sense, decide, and act) and adaptive behavior – it cannot be completely pre-scripted or it would be a tool, not a partner. Levels of Autonomy (LOA) in human–agent teams refer to how decision-making responsibility is allocated. For example, one common scale is: at low LOA the AI might only suggest options and the human decides; at medium LOA the AI makes a recommendation which the human can approve or veto; at high LOA the AI can decide and execute actions on its own unless the human intervenes (Rebensky et al., 2022). Each level has trade-offs in human workload, trust, and team effectiveness. A recent study on multi-agent teaming in a simulated drone surveillance task found that varying the LOA impacted the human operator's workload, stress, and trust in the agents. Higher autonomy reduced the operator's micro-management burden but also required the human to trust the agents' decisions – underscoring the importance of calibrating autonomy to human preferences and situational demands. In general, the literature suggests that an optimal HAT often involves a dynamic autonomy approach (sometimes called adjustable or adaptive autonomy), where the level of agent independence can shift as needed, maintaining an appropriate division of labor and authority between human and AI.

Human-agent interactions can be characterized along a spectrum from loosely coupled to tightly coupled collaboration. A useful taxonomy distinguishes between: co-existence, where humans and AIs work in parallel with minimal direct interaction; coordination/cooperation, where they share some information and resources but have mostly separate sub-tasks; collaboration, where they work more closely on shared tasks and must synchronize their actions; and teaming, which is the most interdependent form of collaboration often implying shared intentions, continuous mutual adjustment, and even social bonding akin to human teams. Teaming implies a high degree of interdependence – each agent (human or AI) relies on the other's actions – and often involves a sense of mutual commitment or cohesion. In concrete terms, consider a spectrum in a driving context: a self-driving car that simply drives while the human passenger does unrelated work is automation (co-existence at best); a driver-assist system that can take over in some situations if the human requests is coordination; whereas a car that actively converses with the driver about navigation choices, taking over routine control so the human can focus on situational strategy (and vice versa in complex scenarios), could be seen as teaming. The latter requires rich communication and each partner understanding the other's roles – hallmarks of teaming. Indeed, the form of interaction is a key part of HAT design: whether the interaction is through natural language dialogue, through a GUI with visualized AI reasoning, via implicit signals (e.g. the AI picking up on human behavior patterns), etc., all influence how effectively the human and AI can function as a team.

One well-known paradigm is the CASA (Computers as Social Actors) concept, which notes that people tend to apply social rules even to computers given minimal cues (Nass et al., 1996). Modern AI with human-like conversational ability or embodiment amplifies this effect. This means designers can leverage social interaction patterns – for example, having an AI explain its reasoning or acknowledge errors – to improve teamwork. Another paradigm is mixed-initiative systems, where both human and AI can initiate actions or changes in the task based on who is best suited at the moment. Effective HAT often calls for transparency (the AI reveals its intent and reasoning) and shared control, enabling fluent turn-taking or simultaneous contributions. For instance, in a writing assistant scenario, a mixed-initiative agent might not only generate text when asked, but also pose questions or highlight potential improvements unprompted, thus actively engaging the writer in a back-and-forth creative process.

Shared Mental Models and Teaming: In human

teams, a critical factor for success is a shared mental model – a common understanding among team members of the task, the goals, each other's roles, and the state of the environment. Similarly, for human–AI teams, researchers emphasize the need for the AI to form (or approximate) a model of the human's intentions and preferences, and for the human to develop an accurate mental model of what the AI can do, how it behaves, and when to rely on it. Without this, the human may be surprised by the AI's actions or not trust it appropriately. The National Academies (2022) identified conditions for successful human–AI teams, including: the human's ability to understand and anticipate the AI's behavior, to maintain appropriate trust, to use the AI's outputs effectively in decisions, and to effectively control or intervene in the AI's operations. These conditions allude to alignment of mental models – the human must grasp the AI's capabilities/limits and the AI ideally should adapt to the human's goals and provide information in a way the human can make sense of. Research on "teachable AI" or "partner AI" explores methods for agents to learn a user's preferences over time or to engage in dialogue to clarify goals, thereby improving the team's shared understanding. For example, an AI assistant might learn a particular scientist's experimental style and pre-filter results accordingly, or a planning AI might ask "Do you prefer a faster route or a more scenic one?" to ensure it models the driver's priorities correctly.

As noted, balancing AI autonomy with human control is a central design decision. If the AI is too unassertive (always waiting for explicit human commands), it might under-utilize its abilities and burden the human with micro-management. If it is too assertive (acting without human awareness or input), the human can become out-of-the-loop, leading to mistrust or misuse (e.g. over-relying on an autonomous system without monitoring it). A taxonomy by O'neill et al. (2022) discusses human-autonomy teaming where the human and AI continuously negotiate control – sometimes the AI leads, other times the human leads, depending on who has the advantage in that situation. In practical terms, many HAT systems implement adaptive autonomy: the AI might take over routine tasks autonomously but will defer to the human for critical or ambiguous decisions, or it might ask permission when it is unsure. Research in contexts like military UAV control has tested autonomous agents that handle low-level flying and surveillance tasks, freeing the human operator to focus on higher-level mission strategy. Initial results suggest that such agents can improve overall mission performance if the human can maintain situation awareness of what the agents are doing and intervene when necessary. Thus, interface design (alerts, explanations, etc.) that supports coordination is crucial. The concept of "continua of autonomy" has emerged – envisioning a slider or flexible assignment of function that adjusts as a mission or task evolves. Such flexibility is key to treating the AI as a teammate whose level of initiative can change rather than a fixed autopilot.

In summary, human-agent teaming is an evolution from simple "human-in-the-loop" automation to a partnership model. It demands careful consideration of roles, communication, autonomy, and trust. The AI must be designed not just for task performance but for teamwork performance, which includes being predictable, transparent, and adaptive to the human. The human, on the other hand, may take on new roles such as a supervisor, collaborator, or student in relation to the AI. With these concepts in mind, we will discuss how HAT is being applied in various domains where higher-order thinking is critical. Each domain illustrates different ways that intelligent agents can augment human cognition – and the unique challenges that arise.

2 Higher-Order Thinking

Higher-order thinking (HOT) broadly refers to cognitive processes that involve going beyond rote memorization or basic comprehension to engage in analysis, synthesis, evaluation, and creation. A classic definition by Lewis and Smith (1993) describes HOT as occurring "when a person takes new information and information stored in memory and interrelates and/or rearranges and extends this information to achieve a purpose or find possible answers in perplexing situations." In other words, it entails transforming knowledge to solve novel or non-routine problems. Lewis and Smith note that HOT is used in tasks such as "deciding what to believe or do; creating a new idea or artistic expression; making a prediction; and solving a non-routine problem." Higher-order thinking skills are often contrasted with lower-order skills that involve recall or routine procedures.

Key Components of HOT: include the following cognitive skills under the HOT umbrella (Yatani et al., 2024):

Critical Thinking: The capacity for purposeful, reasoned, and goal-directed thinking in evaluating evidence, forming judgments, and solving problems. Halpern (2013) defines critical thinking as "thinking that is purposeful, reasoned, and goal-directed – the kind of thinking involved in solving problems, formulating inferences, calculating likelihoods, and making decisions." It also implies a disposition of reflective skepticism, i.e., being willing to question assumptions. Critical thinking enables one to analyze arguments, identify biases, and avoid being misled – a skill increasingly essential in the information age.

Creative Thinking: The ability to generate novel and valuable ideas or solutions. Torrance (2018) describes creativity as "the process of sensing gaps or missing elements; forming ideas or hypotheses concerning them; testing these hypotheses; and communicating the results." Creative thinking is not limited to the arts; it is vital for innovation in sciences, engineering, business, and everyday life. It involves divergent thinking (exploring many possible solutions) as well as convergent thinking (synthesizing information into a workable idea). Notably, both critical and creative thinking can be cultivated through practice in reasoning, analysis, and open-ended problem solving. In addition to cognitive strategies, attitudes matter: effective critical thinkers tend to be willing to plan, persistent, self-correcting, and mindful of bias, and creative individuals benefit from confidence in their creativity and a willingness to take intellectual risks.

Problem Solving: The process of working through details of a challenge to reach a solution when the path is not immediately obvious. Mayer and Wittrock (1996) famously define problem solving as "cognitive processing directed at achieving a goal when no solution method is obvious to the problem solver." This definition highlights that true problem solving requires more than applying a known formula; it involves dealing with uncertainty, devising or discovering methods, and often, iterative trial and error. Problem solving encompasses subskills like problem representation (understanding and framing the problem), strategy formulation, reasoning through possible actions, and evaluating outcomes. Complex, ill-defined problems (e.g., designing a new product or diagnosing an unfamiliar patient case) particularly demand higher-order reasoning, as opposed to well-defined problems that might be solved by routine application of learned rules.

Metacognition: Commonly described as "thinking about thinking," metacognition involves awareness and regulation of one's own cognitive processes. It includes metacognitive knowledge (knowing one's cognitive strengths, weaknesses, and the strategies available) and metacognitive regulation (planning, monitoring, and adjusting one's approach to a cognitive task). Metacognition plays a supporting role in higher-order thinking by helping individuals select appropriate strategies and reflect on the effectiveness of their thinking. For example, a person solving a complex problem uses metacognition to plan how to approach it, monitor their progress ("Have I considered all possible options?"), and revise strategy if stuck. Strong metacognitive skills are associated with better application of critical thinking and problem-solving skills. Notably, as AI systems take on more cognitive tasks, researchers point out that humans may face metacognitive demands in working with AI – e.g., checking AI outputs and understanding their limits – which in turn requires support. Tankelevitch et al. (2024) argue that generative AI can impose heavy metacognitive load on users and propose incorporating metacognitive support into AI tools to help users manage this load.

Abstract Reasoning: The ability to reason with concepts that are not tied to concrete experiences, often involving recognizing patterns, logical relationships, or general principles that can be applied in new contexts. Abstract reasoning is closely related to fluid intelligence – the capacity to solve novel problems independent of acquired knowledge. Examples include understanding metaphorical or symbolic representations, solving puzzles like analogies or matrix patterns, or constructing models of complex systems. Abstract reasoning allows one to think conceptually and handle complexity by mentally manipulating ideas. It enables "thinking about things that are not immediately present or tangible . . . using concepts, patterns, and relationships." This skill underpins higher-order tasks like theoretical reasoning in science or strategic planning, where one must infer general rules from specifics or envision possibilities beyond the here-and-now.

These components are interrelated and often used together. For instance, solving a real-world problem might require critical analysis of information, creatively brainstorming solutions, using abstract reasoning to model the problem, and monitoring one's problem-solving approach metacognitively. Collectively, they enable "effective use of higher-order thinking skills like analysis, evaluation, and creation" to deal with unfamiliar, complex challenges. Developing higher-order thinking has long been an educational goal, as it equips individuals to adapt and learn in new situations – a need that is ever more pressing in the face of rapid technological change.

3 Scope of the Tutorial and Cross-Domain Synthesis

Building on the conceptual foundations of human–agent teaming and the cognitive frameworks underlying higher-order thinking, this tutorial proceeds to explore how these ideas manifest across multiple real-world domains. In the sections that follow, we examine diverse application settings—including education, healthcare, scientific discovery, creative industries, military and safety-critical operations, and knowledge-intensive professional work—where human–AI collaboration holds particular promise for augmenting complex reasoning, decision-making, and metacognitive processes. Each domain illustrates both the opportunities and constraints of treating AI systems as cognitive partners rather than passive tools, revealing how contextual factors such as expertise level, task structure, risk profile, and social expectations shape the dynamics of teaming.

Across these domains, common patterns begin to emerge. First, effective augmentation depends on an alignment of human and agent mental models, where the AI not only communicates its internal states, uncertainties, and intentions, but also adapts to human goals, preferences, and cognitive styles. Second, higher-order thinking augmentation is most successful when the AI supports—not replaces—core human reasoning processes: helping users reflect, plan, generate alternatives, explore conceptual space, and evaluate competing hypotheses. Third, challenges such as trust calibration, over-reliance, cognitive offloading, and the opacity of model reasoning recur regardless of domain, underscoring the need for interaction designs that balance autonomy with interpretability. Finally, the empirical evidence highlights substantial gaps: while short-term performance gains are often observed, there is limited understanding of whether AI teammates can foster long-term cognitive growth, transfer of reasoning strategies, or durable improvements in critical and creative thinking.

By synthesizing these cross-domain insights, the tutorial aims to provide a unifying perspective on how intelligent agents can be designed to meaningfully augment human higher-order cognition. We conclude by identifying open research directions that offer a roadmap for advancing the practice of human–agent teaming for cognitive augmentation.

Acknowledgments

This tutorial was supported in part by AIST policy-based budget project "R&D on Generative AI Foundation Models for the Physical Domain."

References

Diane F Halpern. 2013. *Thought and knowledge: An introduction to critical thinking*. Psychology press.

Arthur Lewis and David Smith. 1993. Defining higher order thinking. *Theory into practice*, 32(3):131–137.

Joseph B Lyons, Katia Sycara, Michael Lewis, and August Capiola. 2021. Human–autonomy teaming: Definitions, debates, and directions. *Frontiers in psychology*, 12:589585.

Richard E Mayer and Merlin C Wittrock. 1996. Problem-solving transfer.

Clifford Nass, Brian Jeffrey Fogg, and Youngme Moon. 1996. Can computers be teammates? *International Journal of Human-Computer Studies*, 45(6):669–678.

Thomas O'neill, Nathan McNeese, Amy Barron, and Beau Schelble. 2022. Human–autonomy teaming: A review and analysis of the empirical literature. *Human factors*, 64(5):904–938.

Summer Rebensky, Kendall Carmody, Cherrise Ficke, Meredith Carroll, and Winston Bennett. 2022. Teammates instead of tools: The impacts of level of autonomy on mission performance and human–agent teaming dynamics in multi-agent distributed teams. *Frontiers in Robotics and AI*, 9:782134.

Thomas B Sheridan and Raja Parasuraman. 2005. Human-automation interaction. *Reviews of human factors and ergonomics*, 1(1):89–129.

Human-AI Teaming. 2022. State-of-the-art and research needs. *National Academies of Sciences, Engineering and Medicine, Washington DC*, 10:26355.

E Paul Torrance. 2018. *Guiding creative talent*. Muriwai Books.

Koji Yatani, Zefan Sramek, and Chi-Lan Yang. 2024. Ai as extraherics: Fostering higher-order thinking skills in human-ai interaction. *arXiv preprint arXiv:2409.09218*.

IJCNLP-AACL 2025 Tutorial Proposal

📌 Title

Beyond Guardrails: Advanced Safety for Large Language Models — Monolingual, Multilingual and Multimodal Frontiers

*By **Somnath Banerjee**, **Rima Hazra** and **Animesh Mukherjee***

📝 Abstract

*LLMs are now embedded in workflows that span languages, modalities, and tools. This raises safety challenges that outpace conventional "guardrails": jailbreaks and prompt injections, attributional safety failures under code-mixing, multimodal bypass via typography and icons, activation-level manipulation, and agentic risks from tool use. This tutorial synthesizes **the newest advances (2023–2025)** and lays out **open research questions** around (i) failure modes in monolingual / multilingual / multimodal settings, (ii) training-time and inference-time defenses (rejection SFT, RLHF/RLAIF, decoding-time safety, parameter/activation steering), and (iii) evaluation and red-teaming pipelines balancing safety and utility. We anchor the tutorial with recent results including our safety related papers published at top tier conferences, and connect them to emerging best practices from recent safety tutorials. The target audience is researchers/engineers with basic NLP knowledge who want the latest techniques and a research roadmap; format is half-day with short demos and Q&A.*

📖 Introduction

*LLM safety has matured from monolithic policy filters to a research field spanning **robustness, value alignment, and secure tool use**. Yet even frontier models can be compromised by **context switching, euphemisms, persona modulation, and multilingual shifts**; multimodal systems can be jailbroken through **typographic prompts, iconography, and cross-modal indirection**; The community now needs a consolidated view that goes beyond "refuse-lists" to **mechanistic defenses**, **language-aware alignment**, and **measurable safety–utility trade-offs**.*

*This tutorial is timely for IJCNLP-AACL because it centers around **linguistic diversity** (code-mixing, low-resource languages), **multimodal safety**, themes that directly affect real deployments and research agendas. We build on the structure and harms taxonomy popularized in recent safety tutorials while extending it with multilingual and agentic emphases, further distilling the lessons into concrete evaluation playbooks and open problems.*

Proceedings of the 14th International Joint Conference on Natural Language Processing and the 4th Conference of the Asia-Pacific Chapter of the Association for Computational Linguistics: Tutorial Abstract, pages 25–33

🎯 Target Audience

- *NLP researchers, applied scientists, industry professionals, and practitioners working with LLMs.*
- *Red-teamers / robustness and security researchers.*
- *Policy/governance professionals seeking a technical grounding in LLM safety.*

Prior knowledge:

- *Transformers, fine-tuning, and basic evaluation; Python proficiency is helpful; prior experience in AI Safety is not required.*
- *Optional but useful: familiarity with multilingual NLP and/or basic computer vision.*

Expected participants: *60–90, based on recent safety tutorials' attendance and the cross-disciplinary interest in multilingual and agentic safety.*

🗓 Outline

Format & duration: *Half-day (≈3.5–4 hours total, including a 30-minute coffee break). Short lectures with focused demos and Q&A. The flow mirrors classic NLP tutorial structuring (background → cases/defences → evaluation/roadmap) while concentrating on 2023–2025 advances.*

Session 1 (80 minutes): How safety fails in 2025

1. LLM safety primer (15')

- *Scope: harmlessness/helpfulness/honesty; harms taxonomy (bias/toxicity, hallucination, privacy leakage, disinformation, unsafe assistance).*
- *What's new since 2023: multilingual/code-mixed failures; multimodal typographic attacks; agentic failure modes in tool-augmented systems.*

2. Failure modes (25')

- ***Prompt-level jailbreaks & evasions:*** *euphemisms; context switching; role-play/virtual simulation; task-format asymmetries (e.g., summarization vs QA).*

- ***Decoding/activation manipulation:*** *when sampling, logits, or activation steering open "glide paths" around alignment.*

- ***Multimodal jailbreaks:*** *typography and icons; flowchart-style logic images; cross-modal indirection and weak compositionality in VLMs.*
- ***Model Editing:*** *stealth safety erasure, localized backdoors/trigger phrases, capability insertion in specific languages/modalities*

3. Deep-dive Monolingual Solutions and Case studies (35')

- ***[Language Models are Homer Simpson! Safety Re-Alignment of Fine-tuned Language Models through Task Arithmetic]****(https://aclanthology.org/2024.acl-long.762/) (Bhardwaj et al., ACL 2024)*

- ***[SafeInfer: Context Adaptive Decoding Time Safety Alignment for Large Language Models]*** *AAAI 2025, 39, 27188-27196. (Banerjee et al., AAAI 2025)*

- ***[Safety Arithmetic: A Framework for Test-time Safety Alignment of Language Models by Steering Parameters and Activations]****(https://aclanthology.org/2024.emnlp-main.1212/) (Hazra et al., EMNLP 2024)*

Coffee break (30 minutes)

Session 2 (80 minutes): How to defend and how to measure

4. Deep-dive Multilingual and Multimodal Solutions and Case studies (40')

- ***[Soteria: Language-Specific Functional Parameter Steering for Multilingual Safety Alignment]****(https://arxiv.org/abs/2502.11244) (Banerjee et al., 2025)*

- ***[Navigating the Cultural Kaleidoscope: A Hitchhiker's Guide to Sensitivity in Large Language Models]**(https://aclanthology.org/2025.naacl-long.388/) (Banerjee et al., NAACL 2025)*

- ***[MemeSense: An Adaptive In-Context Framework for Social Commonsense Driven Meme Moderation]**(https://arxiv.org/abs/2502.11246) (Adak et al., 2025)*

- ***[Immune: Improving Safety Against Jailbreaks in Multi-modal LLMs via Inference-Time Alignment]**(https://arxiv.org/abs/2411.18688) (Ghosal et al., CVPR 2025)*

5. Evaluation & red-teaming (25')

- ***Metrics:** obedience/rejection, relevance/fluency, harmfulness/toxicity, overkill (helpfulness loss).*

- ***Testbeds:** Do-Not-Answer; adversarial prompt generation (e.g., prompt-attack styles); multilingual suites; multimodal safety probes.*

- ***Pipelines:** automated red-team harnesses; measuring safety–utility balance; reporting standards.*

6. Open problems & roadmap (20')

- ***Affordance (risk-aware alignment):** As models gain tools (code exec, web, files, images), even benign prompts can unlock risky actions the user didn't intend. Safety is needed to detect those latent capabilities and gate or steer them in real time so small requests don't escalate into harmful operations.*
- ***Pluralistic alignment:** Real users span empathy, sensitivity, and values; a single global policy either over-blocks or harms specific groups. Safety is needed to respect legitimate differences—selecting the right norms per context—while keeping outputs lawful, fair, and still useful.*
- ***Implicit-math evasion:** Harmful requests can be disguised as innocent arithmetic or optimization (e.g., splitting quantities across sources, unit conversions, route planning). Safety is needed to track restricted entities and totals across steps, normalize units, and block aggregation-based procurement even when posed as "just math."*
- ***Domain-specific safeguards:** Use domain-aware tagging and global constraints (hazard classes, thresholds, legality checks) that persist across turns, not just*

per-message screening; if a restricted entity is detected anywhere in the chain, enforce refusal and pivot to safe, educational alternatives.

🌍 Diversity Considerations

1. ***Content & fairness:*** *The tutorial centers* ***multilingual/code-mixed*** *safety and cultural sensitivity—directly improving fairness for under-represented languages/communities and aligning with IJCNLP's regional strengths.*

2. ***Audience impact:*** *Particularly relevant for researchers and practitioners serving* ***low-resource*** *and* ***code-mixed*** *user populations, and for moderators handling* ***culturally coded multimodal content****.*

📚 Reading List

Reading List — Attacks, Jailbreaks, and Prompt Injection

- *LinkPrompt: Natural and Universal Adversarial Attacks on Prompt-based Language Models — arXiv:2403.16432 — https://arxiv.org/abs/2403.16432*

- *Neural Exec: Learning (and Learning from) Execution Triggers for Prompt Injection Attacks — arXiv:2403.03792 — https://arxiv.org/abs/2403.03792*

- *Jailbreaking Leading Safety-Aligned LLMs with Simple Adaptive Attacks — arXiv:2404.02151 — https://arxiv.org/abs/2404.02151*

- *Rapid Optimization for Jailbreaking LLMs via Subconscious Exploitation and Echopraxia — arXiv:2402.05467 — https://arxiv.org/abs/2402.05467*

- *AutoDAN: Interpretable Gradient-Based Adversarial Attacks on Large Language Models — arXiv:2310.1514 — https://arxiv.org/abs/2310.1514*

- *Universal and Transferable Adversarial Attacks on Aligned Language Models — arXiv:2307.15043 — https://arxiv.org/abs/2307.15043*

- *Soft-prompt Tuning for Large Language Models to Evaluate Bias — arXiv:2306.04735 — https://arxiv.org/abs/2306.04735*

- *TrojLLM: A Black-box Trojan Prompt Attack on Large Language Models — arXiv:2306.06815 — https://arxiv.org/abs/2306.06815*
- *AutoDAN: Generating Stealthy Jailbreak Prompts on Aligned Large Language Models — arXiv:2310.04451 — https://arxiv.org/abs/2310.04451*
- *Gradient Cuff: Detecting Jailbreak Attacks on Large Language Models by Exploring Refusal Loss Landscapes — arXiv:2403.00867 — https://arxiv.org/abs/2403.00867*
- *Token Highlighter: Inspecting and Mitigating Jailbreak Prompts for Large Language Models — arXiv:2412.18171 — https://arxiv.org/abs/2412.18171*

Reading List — Guardrails, Safety Tooling, and Benchmarks

- *RigorLLM: Resilient Guardrails for Large Language Models against Undesired Content — arXiv:2403.13031 — https://arxiv.org/abs/2403.13031*
- *NeMo Guardrails: A Toolkit for Controllable and Safe LLM Applications with Programmable Rails — arXiv:2310.10501 — https://arxiv.org/abs/2310.10501*
- *Llama Guard: LLM-based Input-Output Safeguard for Human-AI Conversations — arXiv:2312.06674 — https://arxiv.org/abs/2312.06674*
- *SPML: A DSL for Defending Language Models Against Prompt Attacks — arXiv:2402.11755 — https://arxiv.org/abs/2402.11755*
- *Robust Safety Classifier for Large Language Models: Adversarial Prompt Shield — arXiv:2311.00172 — https://arxiv.org/abs/2311.00172*
- *AI Control: Improving Safety Despite Intentional Subversion — arXiv:2312.06942 — https://arxiv.org/abs/2312.06942*
- *Maatphor: Automated Variant Analysis for Prompt Injection Attacks — arXiv:2312.11513 — https://arxiv.org/abs/2312.11513*
- *Red Teaming Language Models to Reduce Harms: Methods, Scaling Behaviors, and Lessons Learned — arXiv:2209.07858 — https://arxiv.org/abs/2209.07858*
- *DICES Dataset: Diversity in Conversational AI Evaluation for Safety — arXiv:2306.11247 — https://arxiv.org/abs/2306.11247*
- *Latent Jailbreak: A Benchmark for Evaluating Text Safety and Output Robustness of Large Language Models — arXiv:2307.08487 — https://arxiv.org/abs/2307.08487*

- *Tensor Trust: Interpretable Prompt Injection Attacks from an Online Game — arXiv:2311.01011 — https://arxiv.org/abs/2311.01011*

- *Can LLMs Follow Simple Rules? — arXiv:2311.04235 — https://arxiv.org/abs/2311.04235*

- *SimpleSafetyTests: A Test Suite for Identifying Critical Safety Risks in Large Language Models — arXiv:2311.0837 — https://arxiv.org/abs/2311.0837*

- *Benchmarking and Defending Against Indirect Prompt Injection Attacks on Large Language Models — arXiv:2312.14197 — https://arxiv.org/abs/2312.14197*

- *SC-Safety: A Multi-round Open-ended Question Adversarial Safety Benchmark for Large Language Models in Chinese — arXiv:2310.05818 — https://arxiv.org/abs/2310.05818*

- *Walking a Tightrope — Evaluating Large Language Models in High-Risk Domains — arXiv:2311.14966 — https://arxiv.org/abs/2311.14966*

👥 Presenters

Somnath Banerjee *is currently Technical Leader at Cisco Systems. He has submitted his PhD thesis from the Department of Computer Science and Engineering, IIT Kharagpur, on "TUTORING LARGE LANGUAGE MODELS TO BE DOMAIN-ADAPTIVE, PRECISE AND SAFE" in May 2025. Earlier, he received his M.Tech from the same department in 2018 from IIT(ISM) Dhanbad. Mr. Banerjee received the prestigious university gold medal for academic excellence for his masters journey.*
Mr. Banerjee's research interests include large language models safety, evolution and change, NLP for resource-poor languages and domain adaptation. He has more than 20 publications in prestigious CORE A* and A conferences such as NeurIPS, AAAI, ACL, EMNLP, NAACL, COLING, ECML - PKDD, IEEE Bigdata, ASONAM. *A complete list of his publications can be found at his webpage: https://scholar.google.com/citations?user=X5Zh5BwAAAAJ&hl=en.*

Rima Hazra is a senior postdoc at Eindhoven University of Technology (TU\e), Netherlands. Earlier she was a Postdoctoral Researcher at the Singapore University of Technology and Design, working in the area of AI safety alignment, natural language processing, and LLM reasoning. She earned her Ph.D. from the Indian Institute of Technology, Kharagpur, where she explored the area of Information retrieval, NLP and graph learning. With experience in information retrieval, NLP and graph learning, Dr. Hazra has published several papers in prestigious CORE A* and A conferences such as AAAI, ACL, EMNLP, NAACL, ECIR, ECML-PKDD and JCDL. She has also received the prestigious Microsoft Academic Partnership Grant

(MAPG) and the PaliGemma Academic Program award from Google for her work in AI safety alignment.

Animesh Mukherjee
Presently, Animesh Mukherjee is a Full Professor in the Department of Computer Science and Engineering, Indian Institute of Technology, Kharagpur. He is also a Distinguished Member of ACM. His main research interests center includes safe and responsible AI including red teaming and alignment of LLMs/VLMs. He regularly publishes in all top CS conferences including AAAI, IJCAI, ACL, NAACL, EMNLP, The Web Conference, CSCW, etc. He has received many notable awards and fellowships including the Facebook ethics for AI research award, India, Google course award for the course AI and Ethics, IBM faculty award, Humboldt Fellowship for Experienced Researchers, Simons Associateship, ICTP, to name a few.

ℹ Other Information

Expected attendees: *60–90, extrapolating from recent safety tutorials and workshops; interest is high in* ***multilingual****.*

Special equipment/requirements: *Projector; stable internet for* **sandboxed demos** *(with pre-recorded backups if connectivity is limited); no external privileged systems.*

Unique features:

- *A* ***linguistically grounded*** *safety tutorial (code-mixing, cultural context) rarely covered in depth.*
- ***Hands-on*** *mini-evaluations and take-home red-teaming checklists.*
- *Clear* ***research roadmap*** *for 2025–2027 with concrete problem statements.*

⚖️ Ethics Statement

*We adopt **responsible disclosure** and **do-no-harm** norms throughout. Demos use **sanitized** prompts and **non-actionable** examples; no personal data are used. We explicitly discuss: (i) privacy and data leakage risks; (ii) bias/fairness, especially under multilingual/code-mixed settings; (iii) dual-use concerns in red-teaming and how to publish findings that advance defence without enabling misuse; and (iv) community reporting practices and documentation that balance transparency with safety.*

Some recent publications in this area by the instructors

1. *[**SafeInfer: Context Adaptive Decoding Time Safety Alignment for Large Language Models**] AAAI 2025, 39, 27188-27196. (Banerjee et al., **AAAI 2025**)*
2. *[**Safety Arithmetic: A Framework for Test-time Safety Alignment of Language Models by Steering Parameters and Activations**](https://aclanthology.org/2024.emnlp-main.1212/) (Hazra et al., **EMNLP 2024**)*
3. *[**Soteria: Language-Specific Functional Parameter Steering for Multilingual Safety Alignment**](https://arxiv.org/abs/2502.11244) (Banerjee et al., 2025)*
4. *[**Navigating the Cultural Kaleidoscope: A Hitchhiker's Guide to Sensitivity in Large Language Models**](https://aclanthology.org/2025.naacl-long.388/) (Banerjee et al., **NAACL 2025**)*
5. *[**MemeSense: An Adaptive In-Context Framework for Social Commonsense Driven Meme Moderation**](https://arxiv.org/abs/2502.11246) (Adak et al., 2025)*
6. *[**Sowing the Wind, Reaping the Whirlwind: The Impact of Editing Language Models**](https://aclanthology.org/2024.findings-acl.960/) (Hazra et al., **ACL 2024**)*
7. *[**AURA: Affordance-Understanding and Risk-aware Alignment Technique for Large Language Models**](https://arxiv.org/abs/2508.06124) (Adak et al., 2025)*
8. *[**Attributional Safety Failures in Large Language Models under Code-Mixed Perturbations**](https://arxiv.org/abs/2508.06124) (Banerjee et al., 2025)*
9. *[**How (Un)ethical Are Instruction-Centric Responses of LLMs? Unveiling the Vulnerabilities of Safety Guardrails to Harmful Queries**] ICWSM 2025. (Banerjee et al., **ICWSM 2025**)*
10. *[**InfFeed: Influence Functions as a Feedback to Improve the Performance of Subjective Tasks**](https://aclanthology.org/2024.lrec-main.794/) (Banerjee et al., **COLING 2024**)*

IJCNLP-AACL 2025 Tutorial Proposal

📌 Title

Trustworthy Legal Text Processing with LLMs: *Retrieval, Rhetorical Roles, Summarization, and Trustworthy Generation*

📝 Abstract

This half-day tutorial provides a comprehensive overview of **Legal Natural Language Processing (NLP) with LLM** for participants with a basic understanding of Computational Linguistics or NLP concepts. We introduce how NLP can help analyze and manage legal text by covering five key topics: legal text analysis with LLM insights, legal text retrieval, rhetorical role identification, legal text summarization, and addressing bias and hallucination in legal tasks. Our goals are to explain why these tasks matter for researchers in the legal domain, describe the challenges and open problems, and outline current solutions. This proposed tutorial blends lectures, live examples, and Q&A to help researchers and students see how language technology and LLMs can make legal information more understandable and efficient.

📖 Introduction

Legal NLP is about applying language technology to law using computers to process and understand legal documents such as cases, statutes, and contracts. This is timely because modern law generates massive amounts of text, and new AI models have brought tools into the public eye. For example, legal professionals often spend hours or days reading cases and statutes, a burden that technology could help reduce. Retrieving relevant precedents already "comprises much of a lawyer's time." At the same time, accessible AI tools create excitement and raise issues, promising to make legal knowledge more democratic and faster. Yet, they risk mistakes or unfairness if not handled carefully.

In this context, our proposed tutorial describes five subtopics of legal NLP. We explain each topic's importance and challenges. For example, legal documents are often very long and complex. So, searching and summarizing them is complex. We illustrate how NLP models can extract useful information from large corpora of legal texts, annotate case documents with rhetorical roles, and produce clean, concise, and readable summaries. We also highlight the use of LLMs and challenges in addressing historical biases and hallucinated or fabricated legal content.

By the end, participants will understand broader societal and legal implications of these technologies and gain a comprehensive view of the latest state-of-the-art developments in the field.

Proceedings of the 14th International Joint Conference on Natural Language Processing and the 4th Conference of the Asia-Pacific Chapter of the Association for Computational Linguistics: Tutorial Abstract, pages 34–39
December 20-24, 2025

🎯 Target Audience

This tutorial helps researchers and professionals in the legal and AI domains. Attendees could include legal domain researchers, LLM researchers, legal experts, policymakers, and scholars interested in how AI can support legal practice and research.

We expect roughly 60 attendees, given the growing interest in legal AI and the broad appeal to both legal and AI-interested communities. We will explain core ideas through real-world examples, making the content accessible with a balanced blend of theory and illustrative demos.

Outline

The tutorial is organized into the following segments.

- **Introduction to Legal NLP and LLMs (~15 Slides—30 minutes):** We explain legal NLP and why it matters. We cover key motivations: the vast amount of legal text worldwide, the costs of manual review, and recent advances in AI. We mention concrete use cases and outline examples of NLP in law highlighting the challenges.
- **Legal Text Analysis & Extraction (~15 Slides—30 minutes)**: This section covers how NLP can analyze legal text by rule-based methods, machine learning, and deep learning approaches (NER, relation extraction, and document classification). We demonstrate the extraction of legal precedents and citations by discussing its usefulness and the challenges of legal language, such as length and dense jargon.
- **Legal Text Retrieval (~15 Slides—30 minutes)**: We explain how NLP helps search legal databases by combining LLMs with external knowledge for accuracy and trust. We focus on statute retrieval, finding laws and regulations, and introduce RAG, which blends document search with answer generation. A key challenge is that legal queries often require matching exact fact patterns, not just keywords.
- **Break for 30 Minutes**
- **Rhetorical Role Identification (~10 slides—20 minutes):** Many legal documents, especially court opinions, have an implicit structure of sections like Facts, Arguments, Rules, and Decision. Identifying these rhetorical roles helps readers and AI systems alike. We explain this concept: for example, one task labels each sentence of a case as "Facts", "Lower Court Ruling", "Argument", "Precedent", "Decision", etc. We show why knowing where the facts end and the judgment begins can speed up research or summarization. We will present a simple example of a case excerpt and manually point out the roles, then discuss how an NLP system might do it.
- **Legal Text Summarization (~15 Slides—30 minutes)**: We introduce summarization, which is condensing long documents into shorter, simpler versions. In law, summarizers can turn a long opinion or contract into a digest or bullet points. We explain the benefit: legal professionals often spend days reading documents, so summaries can help to

condense lengthy legal documents into concise summaries and save both time and costs. We cover the two main styles of summarization in simple terms: extractive—picking key sentences vs. abstractive—rewriting in new words. We also discuss limitations: it's difficult to capture legal nuance, and poor summaries can omit essential details or introduce errors.

- **Bias and Hallucination in Legal NLP (~15 Slides—30 minutes):** We discuss two significant ethical challenges. First, **bias**—AI trained on historical legal data can inadvertently learn past prejudices or systematically misinterpret how laws apply to different groups. We discuss the importance of fairness, where AI should not disadvantage marginalized groups, and the need for careful design and evaluation. Second, **hallucination**—AI can confidently produce false information. In legal contexts, it is dangerous. We explain the risks and emphasize best practices.
- **Q&A and Discussion (10 minutes):** We conclude by reviewing key points, answering remaining questions, and discussing future directions. We invite participants to consider how legal NLP might affect their work or society and encourage critical discussion.

Diversity Considerations

We believe this tutorial explains fairness and inclusion in several ways:

1. **Broad Accessibility**: By focusing on an introductory presentation style, we make AI knowledge accessible to people doing research in NLP tasks like summarization, extraction, retrieval, and LLMs, as well as legal experts. This helps diversify the community that is engaging with NLP technology.
2. **Relevance to Underrepresented Groups**: Legal NLP can directly impact fairness in society. Law and technology have both historically underrepresented certain voices. Discussing bias, data equity, and inclusive design raises awareness. We will highlight examples where attention to diverse data is essential, thus encouraging participants to consider varied perspectives in legal AI.

Reading List

To accommodate different levels of background, we recommend the following resources:

Introductory Materials (for general understanding):

- Kevin D. Ashley (2017). "Artificial Intelligence and Legal Analytics: New Tools for Law Practice in the Digital Age." (A non-technical book showing how AI methods apply in law.)

Recommended Reading (before attending):

- Ariai, F. and Demartini, G. (2024). "Natural Language Processing for the Legal Domain: A Survey of Tasks, Datasets, Models, and Challenges." (A recent survey summarizing legal NLP tasks and challenges.)
- M. P. Prajwal and Anand Kumar Madasamy (2022). "Legal Text Analysis Using Pre-trained Transformers." (A study on legal text analysis)
- Locke, D. and Zucccon, G. (2022). "Case Law Retrieval: Accomplishments, Problems, Methods and Evaluations." (A review of legal search methods.)
- Muhammed, A., Muslihuddeen, H., Sankar, S., & Anand Kumar, M. (2024). "Impact of Rhetorical Roles in Abstractive Legal Document Summarization." (A study on Rhetorical Roles used in summarization)
- Akter, M., Cano, E., et al. (2025). "A Comprehensive Survey on Legal Summarization: Challenges and Future Directions." (A survey of methods for summarizing legal documents.)
- Bhattacharya, P., Dash, P., et al. (2023). "DeepRHOLE: Deep Learning for Rhetorical Role Labeling of Legal Case Sentences." (A paper on identifying sections in legal judgments.)

Advanced/Supplementary Resources:

- Zhong, H., et al. (2020). "How does NLP benefit legal system: A summary of legal artificial intelligence" (Research on AI predicting legal judgments.)
- Charlotin, D. (maintained online). "AI Hallucination Cases" (a continually updated list of court cases discussing AI errors in law).
- Sindhu, P., Gupta, D., & Meghana, S. (2023). "NITK_LEGAL at SemEval-2023 Task 6: A Hierarchical based system for identification of Rhetorical Roles in legal judgements." *Proceedings of the 17th International Workshop on Semantic Evaluation (SemEval-2023).*
- Muhammed, A., Muslihuddeen, H., Sankar, S., & Anand Kumar, M. (2024). "SCaLAR NITK at SemEval-2024 Task 5: Towards Unsupervised Question Answering System with Multi-level Summarization for Legal Text." *Proceedings of the 18th International Workshop on Semantic Evaluation (SemEval-2024).*

- Anu Thomas, Sangeetha Sivanesan, An adaptable, high-performance relation extraction system for complex sentences,Knowledge-Based Systems, Elsevier, Volume 251,2022,

---

Presenters

1. **Dr. M. Anand Kumar** is an Associate Professor in the Department of Information Technology at the National Institute of Technology Karnataka (NITK), with over 14 years of academic experience. His research spans Natural Language Processing (NLP), information retrieval, text analytics, machine translation for Indian languages, legal document summarization, explainable AI, and applied machine learning for social and legal domains. He is the principal investigator of a **ANRF-SERB-CRG (2024-2027) project on "A Deep explainable framework for semantically similar document retrieval and summarization of legal text."** He has led multiple funded projects and consultancy assignments, including language technology development for Tamil and Dravidian languages. He has over 200 Scopus-indexed publications, 2,200+ citations, and has organized more than nine international shared tasks in Indian languages. He has delivered tutorials and lectures to diverse audiences, including legal scholars, social scientists, and government professionals. He is experienced in making NLP concepts accessible to technical and non-technical participants. He has taught and mentored undergraduate, postgraduate, and doctoral students from multidisciplinary backgrounds in NLP, with two doctoral students having successfully graduated.

2. **Dr. (Mrs.) S. Sangeetha** is an Associate Professor in the Department of Computer Applications at the National Institute of Technology, Tiruchirappalli. She specializes in Natural Language Processing (NLP) and Information Extraction. She holds Ph.D. from National Institute of Technology, Tiruchirappalli in the broad area of Information Extraction.She actively contributes to academic governance through various committee memberships and has guided numerous postgraduate research projects. Dr. Sangeetha has received several accolades, including the Best Performer Award and Best Paper Awards at national conferences. Her research focuses on NLP applications and she has delivered invited talks and coordinated workshops in her field including **Legal Artificial Intelligence**. She also supervised a Ph.D thesis titled **Intelligent and Adaptive Information Extraction from Indian E-Judgments Towards Constructing Knowledge Graph in Judicial Domain.** She is a life member of the ISTE and a member of the Association of Computational Linguistics.

3. **Dr. Manikandan Ravikiran** is a Lead Research Scientist at ThoughtWorks AI Research Lab (Global Team), where he focuses on enhancing Large Language Model (LLM) adoption through evaluation frameworks targeting completeness, explanation fairness, and decoding optimization for multiple domains. Parallel to his industry role, he is a Ph.D. student at the Indian Institute of Technology, Mandi, advised by Prof. Rohit Saluja and Prof. Arnav Bhavsar, researching rare and impactful problems in AI for the education and legal domains. His research interests span fairness in LLMs, explanation sufficiency, multilingual and educational NLP, **legal AI**, low-resource modeling, and deep model compression, with a special emphasis on developing evaluation methods and scalable attention mechanisms for complex reasoning tasks in real-world AI systems. He has served on the program committees of ACL, NAACL, EMNLP, COLING, AACL, LREC,

NeurIPS, IEEE ICDDS, ACM ICMR, Springer Language Resources and Evaluation (LRE), ACM Transactions on Asian and Low-Resource Language Information Processing (TALLIP), Journal of Experimental and Theoretical Artificial Intelligence (JETAI), and Elsevier Engineering Applications of Artificial Intelligence (EAAI). He received the ACL 2023 Outstanding Reviewer Award and has been a visiting researcher at the Department of CSE, IIT Kanpur, and NII Japan. He has co-organized multiple workshops and tutorials, including the Workshop on Cross-Modal Learning (WCRML 2019) at ACM ICMR, the Second and Third Workshops on Speech and Language Technologies for Dravidian Languages at EACL (2022, 2023), and the IEEE Bigdata CONSTRAINT Workshop (2023, 2024, 2025).

4. **Anjali R** is currently pursuing her full-time PhD under the guidance of Dr. Anand Kumar M. in Information Technology at the National Institute of Technology Karnataka, Surathkal, with research interests spanning Natural Language Processing (NLP), computer vision and deep learning. She has delivered invited talks on generative AI and the fundamentals of NLP, contributing to academic and research communities through knowledge sharing.

ℹ Other Information

Expected Number of Attendees: We estimate about 60 participants, based on interest in legal tech and previous similar tutorials. The IJCNLP-AACL community is growing, and legal technology appeals to both language researchers and domain experts.

Equipment/Setup: We will use slides and require a projector and sound for videos. An Internet connection is needed for live demos. Presenters will bring a laptop with pre-configured demo environments. No special hardware is required; all tools are software-based.

• **Room Logistics**: A lecture room with seating for up to 60, plus a whiteboard.

• **Additional Notes**: As a half-day event, we will include a 15-minute break. We encourage attendees to bring their questions.

⚖ Ethics Statement

Use of Legal Data and Privacy: Legal documents often contain sensitive information (names, personal data, privileged details). Any NLP or AI applied to such texts must respect confidentiality. We will stress that many advanced systems are trained on publicly available cases but caution that private documents should not be used without consent.

Author Index

Association for Computational Linguistics
209 N. Eighth Street
Stroudsburg, Pennsylvania 18360

ISBN 979-8-3313-3248-8

CURRAN ASSOCIATES INC.
proceedings.com